SKIRT

By

Sudhir Kumar Aggarwal

Disclaimer

This is a work of poetic fiction. Names, characters, places, institutions and incidents are either the product of author's imagination or are fictitious, and any resemblance to any actual person, living or dead, events or locales is entirely coincidental.

Copyrights

This is original work of the author. All efforts have been taken to make the material error-free. *However, the author disclaims the. responsibility*

Author's Notes

The book is a collection of poems on the theme of SKIRT.

The collection is an exotic concoction of desire, romance, yearning, passion, action, conscious and unconscious, games, imagination and fantasy, with dash of realty.

Mini

I am one with my Mini, skirt
in summer, winter and spring
we in joy, whirl, twirl and swirl
and dance as flying on wings.
Symmetrical hem, bandeau up
a real mini up the legs, high up
of cotton with pleats and light
it whirls up and up the thighs.

We often walk to colony circle
garden, fountain, pole in centre
we walk through perimeter
of square, sides of fifty meters.
We come down the stairs of
our house, up on the balcony
longingly, stands twin brother
wishing I could be friend's sister,
and they would be fast around
within seconds we are found.

We walk few steps and turn left

neighbour, fathers' friend stops
his car, quickly comes beside us
we coolly decline lift, little does
he know, for walk we live and die
to feel wind in, up and up high.
Before that, on last of the stairs
grand old neighbour on other side
says beautiful, pleasant weather, hi!
we whirl, smile, say hello! goodbye.

Boss is there on second left turn
advancing from opposite direction
dazzled, with open mouth, stares
with wide eyes, in less of a second
issue settled forever, who the boss
is, by his pleading eyes, we give
sight full for refreshing his mind.
Recent is story of queer uncle John
when mini spun fast in huge storm
his face turned left, neck stuck right
hope! in other storm return it might.

They are here, all, them claim

your faithful boyfriend, same
that’s enough of wish insane
we have no interest in names
one of them walks close by
foolish, he does what mustn’t
to shield us from roving eyes
he must be punished as soon
how dare he monopolizes moon
if he does look here and there
shall be thoroughly chastised
if he does, I shall change skirt
tomorrow, I am not recognized.
As we take final left turn and
joyfully whirl, twirl and swirl
fast coming bikes skid roadside
as we swirl, gyrate and rotate
speeding cars crash on other side
safe is to walk in centre of road
soon there is crowd all round
we are in middle of a traffic jam
on Mini is all eyes’ direction
as we zigzag find, our way
onwards, world stands still

only we swirl, whirl and twirl.

It is in my Chelsea look,
as in slanted front pocket
I keep the key, forget and
carry world inside, all them
wait with bated breath for a
mighty swirl, twirl and whirl
whoever picks, whenever falls
none to envy, winner takes all.
We are near circle, I see high
my house, behind a window
lurking there familiar shadow
I feel him with deep nigh sigh.
Circle has wind strong as gale
fountain fast jetting water hail
and majestic pole rising up high
all eyes watch for heaven in sky
pleated light lifts high up high
nothing inside, perfect is sight.

Red Skirt

Reacted she
on reading a
poem, obviously
not shared here.

How could!
how could you!
write this poem
of desire.
It has captured
all I ever dreamt
my teenage and
woman desires,
told you just one
unfulfilled desire of
wearing red mini
skirt in public
at age of fourteen.
Even if you know
me well for long
but you can't
see through me
even if present,

but not long past.

Yes, I assure you
nothing of this
you ever told me
none of your
words and phrases
I have interpreted
but it is true
this is my poem
it has stunned you
shocked you
to a bliss that you
can't cope with.

Must be an
unconscious connect
which led to this
from your sharing
of one desire
my desire of you

felt all your desires.

Intensity of feelings

transcended boundaries

of situation, time, space

and from thereon

in few moments

I just penned this.

These are not words,

it is a poem of you

read yourself again

your desire melted me

for moments, me spilled

on paper, it smeared.

Grey Skirt

When I wear skirt ‘n sway

awareness vanishes away

hang it around thighs, high

to the world close eyes.

You were not in classroom
till half time, kicked a broom,
did not wish headmaster
he crossed you in corridor,
hitched on postman's bicycle
scribbled gibberish on wall
pushed a rickshaw uphill
rode behind a tempo, silly!
raced through a red light.

You were playing cricket
with boys and flying kite
went along and had fight
ate buns and drank soda
washed clothes in pond
with washer women, fat
plucked a lotus and sat
on the edge of the river
legs dangling in water,
gulped raw fishes, two
were roaming in orchard
hanging upside down free
from branch of jamun tree,

on return ate in neighbours'
house not visited by us,
when I yelled, you did
not turn and respond,
been hearing about
you this and that
throughout the day,
has been hell of a day
girl! where were you?

Have come back two
hours after the school
your bag left on stool
teacher sent information,
this is not the first time
you have done like this
when you wear grey skirt
you always behave amiss,
shirt is torn and soiled
ink is smeared on skirt
it is muddy, girl behave,
in school wear trousers.

This is what mother told
when I returned home bold
as I was taking off the skirt
could barely hear some of it.
I cannot, when I get in skirt
see self, world is mirror like
in which I get trapped inside
I am there on the other side,
what seen is, image who does
not know this world, and flows
wild, she does what she does.

Mother please understand,
were like me, don't pretend
you look longingly, I know it
when I am to wear the skirt.
You know well, the future
that is a mirage I better live,
steal few hours, from omen,
long struggle, life of women.

Pencil Skirt

Life, an instruction's chart
don't stand legs apart
sit cross legged
take short strides
keep knees covered
to go anywhere, ask
come back early
don't frown, smile,
not knowing
to skirt issues
and to comply
to stay straight
wore Pencil skirt.

It was so tight
there was always
sweat between thighs
not knowing don'ts
could even do's not
could not lift
struggled to climb ladders,
first time fell down

almost broke knee
couldn't do cycling
became game ugly.

Years of sufferings
and   many injuries
on a rough day in anger
exploded on mother
post incident, she added
a pleat in skirt, a relief
some space to move
on another time
yelled at big brother
skirt was slit at back
could walk boldness,
getting hang of way
growing in status
and confidence
confronted father
got slit on both sides
could move with
freedom.

It is still a Pencil skirt
one which I could adjust.
what is written with
pencil can be erased
but life cannot
be rewritten, learn
from Pencil skirt
wear with long slits
not repeat history, skirt.

Skirt Pink

Much before sunrise every day in skirt pink
rush to practice moves in ice skating rink
I look at face in mirror hanging above sink
with sheer delight see on cheeks rosy chink
bubbling with energy come out and sprint
on asphalt road shoes sing and sing, clink
less than four inch, I always wear skirt pink
and a coat mink, few see with awe and blink
some do dare wink, silly them! not to think
we practice as duos, I look for beau klink
he there early perfecting the moves in rink

says, in your absence it is boring and swink
looks longingly, me in micro mini brink pink
I feel me flame, and remove the coat mink
we come together dancing, look and blink
raise my gymnastic thigh touching sky of rink
so rise his infinite, in alignment bodies link
we dance, in and out, dink chink, dink chink
every morning I come, come out, in slink
all eyeballs on verge of coming out brink
it is a daily routine, I wear skirt brink pink
we dance, just dance, dink chink, dink chink.

When to Wear Skirt

Two perfect times to wear skirt
there is or nothing is underneath,
when you wear this one, and you
take it off to wear another one,
want to hide thighs from wind
not to hide shy but unwind,
to loosen up in times of crisis
loose character to avoid crisis,
want to be simple, sophisticated

sweet, sexy and show stopping
want to do this, do that, easy
want to give this, get that, easy
you feel love goddess inside
wish to capture men besides
when you allow in, be yourself
or come out and spill yourself
for any situation there is a skirt
to be successful wear that skirt
really it to be worn two times
at this moment, and lifetime.

How to Wear Skirt

There are simple clues, first is
set own principles, one possible
rule, how good you feel and
impression on others she makes
length is determined by width
width longer than skirt length
hem of skirt is personal pride
how much to reveal and hide
best is highly tantalizing

but allowing no peep inside
is matter of girth and height
your choice adjusts skirt size
skirt is to be well above knees
necessarily with split on thighs
to be dark as much as possible
shine comes from your glamour
should whirl when you stand up
should ride up when sit down
is not mere a piece of clothing
is joy of heart peace of mind
no cloth near around or inside
free space full ventilation beside
necessary to keep things cool
natural fire often happens inside,
exudes feel of sensual you
even best of the minds spoon
lose their head and compete to
take prestige walk to you bow
that is how you wear skirt as
if your destiny it determines
simple test of correct how is
when you wear favourite skirt

you a portrait in vast landscape
all men want to be in the space.

Why to Wear Skirt

Coming to brass tacks, skirt to serve twin purpose
to world rendering messages psychic and physique,
irrelevant is your size, faithful skirt does serve right
wear as if correctly fits, makes you feel damn tight,
whatever height or girth, all women are beautiful
skirt to make women shape of an hourglass figure,
to save time of games, plays of tentative indirect
and to bring attention to centre by looking direct,
capture dilemmas, sheds vulnerability and fright
sends clear message and exudes empowerment
you feel energetic, youthful and revolutionary
unconventional not covert to reveal, liberation
revel in independence, maturity and playfulness
desire to please, condemned to love, exploitation,
looks of Lolita girl, androgynous, prepubescent
figure childish shape, and great deal of long legs
an oxymoron appearance, you feel cool they feel
sexy and vice versa, either way master of universe

you walk and be in skirt as if you to win the world
in doing so have nothing to lose but only your skirt.

Chasing the History of Skirt

From grasses tied to strings
grown to billion dollar rings
not enough to graze for men
stings, poor tied to eternal string
originated for women and men
intelligent quickly choose women,
first outer garment which tells us
what is outside, what under shells
simple cloth easy to stich but is
grossly understated erotic dress,
has been so comfortable some
discomfort has been experimented
long, virtue of modesty and prestige
status of beauty is narrow waistline
skirt design a bit personal style
great possibility to be an individual
multiple shapes, form colour and size

musing, amusing is play with hemline
make women flow be wild, expand
many get immortalized in legends,
skirt symbolizes women, scatter brained
seductive gives her definite upper hand
a pretty gender but not very intelligent
keeps intellect secret as does in skirt.
Skirt means women, a way of dealing
issues of social and global significance
enhancer of below the waist glamour
for ages linked to social temperature
truth or myth of linking to recession
hooking with skirt is men's obsession
skirt changed, for centuries nothing
changed, to El dorado chase unending
earth revolves all times men to unwind
history of skirt is journey of mankind.

How to Skirt

If a man raises issues, stupid
Questions, which he would
asks with impunity such as

number of your boy friends
say hello! with droopy eyes
fellow starts looking down
you swing slowly skirt gyrates
shifts attention forgotten issue is
change conversation stop swing
if one bit intelligent would pick
up new conversation issue gone.

He may be real stupid, swing again
till the fella learns to follow swing
and joins your line of conversation
swing n' swing ensure he is tamed.

Skirt Alternatives

Tried few shorts too tight too loose
under or over length very flat shape
clings or hangs as a separate thing
relegated to casualness loss of identity.
Tried trousers, length too much takes
whole space covers legs lacks grace
feeling of walking   enclosed, trapped

limits ventilation impossible to relate.

Aim of a dress is to feel sun air fresh
feel nature live natural and bond with
the wearer as if two together growing
shining personality, identity evolving.
Tried alternatives, sticking or hanging
either eclipsed or demanded much of me.
All dresses promising but traps in their
structures, lack message of flexibility, care
warmth, however much flirted with dresses
others ultimately reverted to live with skirt.

Life without Skirt

An unusual day, as I get up to calmness
feels eerie silence of ominous morning
humid, lazy, strolling air overwhelming
move I, aimless in room, open curtains
look through window dully sky and dust
emptiness in horizon, deafening silence
as if city woken up after a catastrophe

in distance, indecisive Sun lest forgotten
rising, in limbo, still, to not meet sky, leave
earth, she unwilling sullen and lethargic
Sun fed up of routine of rising and setting
earth tired of its weight rotation on axis
as if energy of cosmos on hold, incomplete
unfulfilled, that is how I found myself awake
in very depressive state without skirt naked.

Skirt and Economy

Hemline length has
direct correlation with
inflation and economy
some believe it a myth
others feel it is true,
let us understand
sample this
hemlines have been
rising and falling
mainly rising
inflation doing
the same
a short skirt saves
cloth and money

it attracts money
has effect on economy
the more it rises
robust is attraction
and flow of money
believe it!
if not
have you ever seen
women in skirt?

On Making

Millions

Oh! pretty
wearer of skirt
cast your spell
on a rich fool
he is bound to
fall flat for you
on his shoulder
shed tears
till he buys
you crocodile
mini skirt.

Skirt and Culture

Tulip skirt is very
popular in west
not in east
is there secret?
All skirts sensitive
to nature tulips
grow full year in west
a month at best in east.
Skirts are culturally
responsive how openly,
boldly and frequently
people visit tulips sites
on that decides skirt
tulip, own popularity.

Skirt and Sky

In canopy of sky humans survives

in the flair of skirt humanity thrives

looking at sky one cannot escape blues

vanish blues, generosity of skirt strikes

sky cause floods, pour both to fertilize

through skirt comes steady stream of life

sky gets clouded unsure of its appearance
as skirts change, emerges new appearance
it is nature but sky know not own nature
inside skirt is known of mysterious nature
which of two is greater, infinite only time
can tell, to hold time, space, greater than the
sky, has to bend, but from time immemorial
in presence of skirt bends world on its own.

Where Heaven Is?

To find address
Skirt is useful
aid for the
purpose
shape of sky
is flair of skirt
to find heaven
you are
to look up
from bottom
of stairs

reaching to sky,
view sky from
telescope
focus between stairs
supported on
two pillars
ahead is figure,
skirty flare
if you find
the centre
peep, in eye
of the sky
you have
heaven's address

Cross Talk with Skirt Lead

Girl in yellow skirt
kept on saying
shall be flying
shall be flying
in short time
kept on waiting

skirt didn’t go up
I asked
looking at skirt
when is it going up?
name plate read
I am Leading Lady
hiding blush stern
her clarification
I am talking
about aircraft
but if you can do
that to aircraft
can’t do same?
I looked at skirt
softly replies
you are in flight
that is what you are
not understanding
retort I, you
misinterpreting
my interest
only if you Lead,
skirt

others' would rise
looking at skirt
behind
of pair of legs.

Sales Girl in Skirt

Gave me hand
made chocolates
in a shining wrapper
matching skirt colour
as I looked at her
smiling she, says
lot of efforts
in making chocolates
is to be slowly put
in mouth
let it melt savour
taste, flavour

Yes! good advice
I usually put inside
swallow quickly bite

glancing at skirt
ask her benignly
looking at her
what do you think
I am doing for
past five minutes
skirt
she smiles swirls skirt
handing over packet
explains! you know Sir
legs are used for making
chocolate paste. Skirt!

Skirt and Chocolate

I always wear skirt
I eat chocolates
start mornings with
a packet of chocolate
the tastiest kind
bean shape and size
today opened in haste
spilled all over me

many went inside top
rubbing me through
sweet chocolates!
most rested over tight skirt
felt one has *gone* inside
chocolate!
could retrieve fifteen
packet says sixteen
sure, one is inside
explored everywhere
could not locate.
felt myself a chocolate!

I live in skirt
like it so much
don't take out
as if I am skirt
I am sixteen
I am a chocolate
let chocolate be
within chocolate
stay where it is
only skirt knows

I am a skirt.

Executive Skirt

Came on purpose in air conditioned spaces
cool air settles down manages centigrade
wearer to be straight, alert and message
other person to be on guard not dart eyes
balance emotion and tasks wearer not to
entice, looker not to get tempted arduous
training on both sides, issue complicated
wearer smart young test really very tight.
Skirt is not to be pursued at any cost it
poses gravest of threat don't ever risk
under rate skirt connections run deepest
could spring roadblocks stall career paths
dull colours of skirt, no indicator of virility
rather is subtle camouflage of vitality
if you look on too often it certainly is a

loosing game, work prestige and skirt one
by one, if don't look remain role straight
then soon win badge of work alcoholic.
Higher you climb more is skirty attention
lesser diversions, fine tune climbing pattern
a test of endurance in garb of endearment
opportunity to conquer, rise to goal highest.

Skirt within Skirt

Woman, a life of beauty
cynosure of every eye
believes, it everlasting
lives enamoured with
doesn't dawn reality
world is full of beauty
glamour, a shade of time
could see elder fading
old in silence weeping
wishes to be ever lasting
woman doesn't awake
time flies beauty fades

dream vanished in seconds

missed life, sighs! skirt.

She of her mothers'

wisdom, prepared

in advance, choose to

wear skirt, only skirt

at all ages of beauty

she and skirt both

together carried her

as beauty in skirt

what women lacked

was made up by skirt

what got lost in skirt

was gained by woman

together they everlasting

at every step skirt adjusting

all call her skirt, she for

herself , skirt with in skirt.

Skirt N' Image

Skirt a humble thing never asserts existence

as soon as one sees, one goes into imagination
thoughts race fast and immediately transport
to far time and spots, the destinations sweetest
of one's past. Imagination dissolves in syrup of
memories, two together a heady concoction.

Or pleasant imagination in time, takes to future
an exotic world of possibilities which is the root
of existence of world. When one stares, skirt
senses and imagines togetherness, joins flight.

Magic happens in moments , as one looks at
other, only for flicker of time, agape, quick auto
scan and natural cycle of imagination complete
humble skirt leaves scene as she of non existence.

Recurring images of skirt forms a sky, a canopy
of sweet feelings inside, in essence there is an
omni presence of skirt in mind, when a person
finds enough solace in images then decides to go
high, climbs, and takes reality tour of imagination
however, much may travel far, but whenever
looks at skirt, immediately gets into an image.

It is the nature of skirt to pose humble existence
to evoke images, encourage reality check and asserts
belongingness and relevance. Let's accept in bliss
skirt is imagination, essence and humanness.

Skirt Fantasy

A tech word, as she feels skirt
goes to sleep it breeds a new
skirt suited for feel of new day.

When she wears skirt everyone
knows she is the one with head
it is they whose head is in it.

They realize skirt wearer is the
gentlest human being, skirt
means respect, they just bow to it.

Skirt a symbol of revolution, when
they feel bold warrior, to show
courage opts to wear a skirt.

Skirt means Princess, of world
magnetic effect greater than earth's
field, partner in spell, bound in skirt.

Skirt, a call of celebration for all
celebrities wear skirt, and those
who wear skirt become celebrities.

Skirt is sex appeal, wearer final
appellate authority, no where
else appeals are admitted.

Skirt designs personal style
and essence, killing proof when
chics your own gender, whistle.

Skirt means epitome of beauty
narrow waist whimsical stunning
obey mesmerised men, feel winning.

Lifting the skirt is unnecessary
skirts made to naturally reveal
on its whiff, lift long pillars.

Revealing is the only norm and
belt skirt is for bold fashion
to revel long in passion.

Everyone can have the cake
world is a damn erotic place
not more than skirt space.

A Prayer

O' Goddess Skirt
give me blessings
that in my dreams
are skirts, only skirts
I chase them and
they skirt me
an endless game
to reach skirts
let me earn daily
bread by winning
each day a new skirt

Two Secrets

I overhear a conversation
between a guy ,an expert
in 'colours and his smart
skirt wearing girl friend
where skirt ends, feels,
caressing her thighs, he
says, here is different tinge,
colour as if red, rosy or pink

but not, what colour is this
and how thighs are so soft .

Replies! it is no shade of pink
nor colour of permanent ink
colour is unique of each thigh
when wears skirt above thigh
woman bold meets men's eyes
by a trill love lacquer rushes
woman's thighs softly blushes
color is of unique wavelength
a new hue, soft becomes thighs.

These are two secrets of skirt; that is
how women' thighs get soft and blush.
Women knowing this rightly fetished
these women destined to be goddess.
If a man can spot the colour difference
any women on earth he can understand
if he can catch each new wavelength' hue
is not far for becoming God, gets the cue.

Skirt Test

O' Skirt

A test to understand you are
a skirt or an intelligent head

Answer straight don't skirt.

Is it ok to be his bit of skirt?
Ok to make him chaser of skirt?
Prefer skirt to intelligent head?
Deal head on, never skirt.
Expert in lifting the skirt?

To how many questions yes
is answer, if there a no is
please wear favourite skirt
switch on natural, reach
quick, temperature of unrest
with renewed vigour take test
O' brave skirt, do your best.

What A Skirt Is, Is Not

It's like asking importance of perception in life
on influence of perception by skirt, runs world,
It is like asking how useful intelligence is
look at skirt, instant answer, useless is intelligence,
It is like asking what is smarter than thinking
one may pretend but skirt is the only thinking,
It is like asking what purpose of chemistry is
in skirty chemistry resides human history,
It is like asking has one been part of history
if understand skirt nothing of life is mystery,
It is like asking how good one is at geography
local or global Skirt is determinant of geography,
It is saying does mathematics anyone understands
skirt holds magic, one plus one equals to world,
It is like asking which is large sky or earth
apt to ask, wider than both, girth space of skirt,
It is like asking how to revolve around earth
would become easier if can run around a skirt,
It is like questioning, is human race not progressing
enter skirt, go straight, there won't be any asking,
better, one might try to ask what a skirt is not
yes, closer, it is a not ,between death and life a knot.

Skirt Day

Like earth there is a divine planet
on it once was declared Skirt Day
warning! read at your own peril
their story is not for faint hearted.
It was agreed after great debate
day be celebrated once in decade
instant transformation happened
and all days became Skirt Days.

Quickly it got resolved impromptu
done away were all dress codes
to tear away workplace stress
for women Mini would be dress
when women not at work, if not
Mini, can wear any other skirt.

Productivity went high phenomenally
work happened fast, vanished quickly
everyone cooperated very motivated
saved time to enjoy skirty magics.

Life total fun, work also fun tweet
honour history, celebrate work week.

Flowers had crush on skirty women
roses blushed, an auspicious omen
magnetic pull of planet was so high
that romantics from grave would rise.
Eve teasing, rape went away vices
people found everything in plenty
there were no crimes no accidents
everyone became nice and decent
there was no punishment, as capital
would have been futile to do firstly
there was no crime secondly a truth
all capital resided in women's skirt.

Men came under the magic spell
hearts of many came out in hand
their minds grew restrained and
on planet, holy peace prevailed.
Rich, powerful got affected most
many left wealth went with skirts

billions vanished without trace
Skirts became only saving grace.
Paternalistic dynasties fell like nine pins
kings saw futility of power, doubts rising
you can't order anyone, would not a force
why to be king, if could do not meek act
none ready to be king, kingdoms vacant
no value without having women in skirt.
Collapsed marriage, similar institutions
relations matter of skirt key encryption.

No dearth of entrepreneurial spirits
through hard work and bit by bit
daring women used skirt to amass
wealth, created harems in weeks.
Any path lead to unlimited riches by
wearing a short skirt, acting sublime
poverty vanished quick, so did famine
plenty to feed in the world feminine.

Unending queues at sex change clinics
long waiting list for license to practice

it is the most held belief of the planet
and advise of wisdom and skirt sane
when time of next Skirt Day comes
on planet only women would remain.
Wonders happened on declaration
of Skirt Day, people stopped ageing
some reversed at lightening pace, in
no time became young adults or teens
formula, each centimetre above thigh
reduced age, by a year, for the elders
soon micro mini became very popular
bold ones made progress in belt skirt.

Education was an unexpected tragedy
looking at and being with bright skirts
minds expanded very fast at young age
luminous insights, teens became bright.
Business got damn easy and simplified
only transactions, no currency or price
such were their algorithmic insights
matters resolved by skirty bright.
Borders of countries were dissolved
a great sign of unity and progress,

there were no army, men, and no guards
mankind solved issues in skirt borders.

Planetary changes happened fast
Venus was understood at last
such was magic of skirty glamour
moon started shining in its reflection
sun went as usual on business but
bright light served no longer purpose,
ocean changed from white and blue
in skirty joy, water glistens as purple
colour of the sky became rainbow
a permanent sight of magic glow
wind became soft and innocent
she blows with divine fragrance
land is as soft as women's thighs
even stones turn to skirts on touch
fire vanished and rested in spaces
where it burns and is never doused
there are only two sounds, laughter
and clamour for Skirt day! Skirt day!
Serious are impacts of celestial nature
would forever change gal axial future

any planet or star getting Skirt planet's
message, would be celebrating Skirt Day.
I could had only glimpse of the planet
forgot to tell its name is new heaven.

About Author

Sudhir Kumar Aggarwal is a generalist Human Resource Professional employed in a large Indian organisation. He has passion for people's development, is accredited and volunteers for Sensitivity Training / Personal Growth Labs. He could be reached at **giftofinsights@gmail.com.**

Made in the USA
Monee, IL
21 October 2026

66035049R00030